SPELLING BEA

Catherine Bruton

Illustrated by **Sarah Hoyle**

OXFORD
UNIVERSITY PRESS

Letter from the Author

I am an award-winning author of stories for young people, including *No Ballet Shoes in Syria* and *We Can be Heroes*. I also teach English and Drama and this story was inspired by one of my pupils, Hester Poole.

Like the amazing Morven, Hester is registered blind, but she has never let that hold her back. She raised £30 000 for Mekele Blind School in Ethiopia, earning her a nomination for the Bond International Development Award which honours outstanding humanitarian work. Hester is a talented singer, actor and athlete. Having recently won a Bronze Medal at the European Paralympic Ski Championships, she hopes to compete in the next Winter Paralympics. All the best bits of this story totally come from Hester!

Catherine Bruton

Chapter One

> **Spelling Rule 1: Qu**
>
> The letter Q is always partnered with the 'silent' letter U. Together they make a 'kw' sound.

Quick. Queen. Quiet. You never see Q without U – that's the rule. They're best friends – one speaks, the other is silent.

Q and U were like Crystal and me. She was the Queen. I was the Quiet One. The Bea (that's my name, Bea, short for Beatrice) to her Queen. 'Queen Bea' they called us – like we were one person. Until she made new friends at the end of Year 4 and told me I was *weird*.

Now I'm just Bea. B. A solitary silent letter like the B in *dumb* and *limb*. People don't even notice it's there.

So I was dreading the first day of term. Going back into Year 5 with no one to sit with, or giggle with, or share lunch with.

'You'll make new friends,' said Mum. But I wasn't sure I knew how to 'make' friends.

Crystal and I had just *been* friends for so long, I'd forgotten how it had happened.

'Isn't there a new girl in your class?' said Mum. 'Just be friendly, smile, ask questions.'

But when I turned up in the classroom, there was no sign of the new girl. Crystal and her friends kept looking at me and giggling.

Ms Moon had stuck a sticky note on the chair next to mine saying: 'Morven'.

Ms Moon told us about Morven before she arrived. The new girl had a vision impairment, which meant she couldn't see very well. Morven didn't have a cane or a guide dog – at least not at school. 'She doesn't want you to treat her differently,' said Ms Moon. 'Just be your usual friendly selves'.

When Morven appeared, you wouldn't have known she had a vision impairment. She bounded into the classroom, found her way to the desk and plopped into the seat next to mine. 'Howdy, partner!' she grinned.

What had Mum said? Smile. Be friendly. Ask a question. 'Hi …' I stammered. 'What's … your name?'

'I'm Morven – obviously!' she laughed.

I could feel myself go bright red and didn't know what to say. While Crystal – and the whole class – stared at me, Ms Moon was talking about an exciting new event that term.

'The Spelling Bee competition is for local schools. The grand prize is £1000 of books for the winning school!'

I tried to concentrate on what she was saying. I love spelling. I like the rules, the patterns, and the fact that you can learn a spelling and it never changes. It stays the same. Not like people.

'We are holding a class competition to select the team today,' Ms Moon explained. 'There will be a written round, then a spoken round.'

I found the written round easy. Next to me, Morven typed her answers on a little machine that looked like a typewriter.

'It makes Braille,' she explained.

'Braille?'

'It's words you can read with your fingers.'

I looked at the series of little raised bumps on the paper.

'Ms Moon has been learning to read it,' said Morven. 'Which is pretty cool – right?'

'The spoken round will be like the real competition,' Ms Moon explained. 'If you get your word wrong, you are out. Last one standing is the winner.'

When I get nervous, my head starts to pound and I can feel myself breathing awkwardly. My first couple of words were easy (*unique, quantity*) but I kept hesitating as I spelled them. I could see Crystal thought I was being weird.

At last, just four of us were left – me, Crystal, Morven and Kevin Henderson.

Queasy was my next word.

I could feel Crystal looking at me, wanting me to get it wrong. I felt like I could hardly breathe.

'Q – E – No! I mean – Q – U –'

The pounding was filling my head and I felt dizzy.

'I'm sorry, Bea. We can only accept your first answer,' said Ms Moon.

'But I know it. Q always goes with U – always!'

I knew my voice came out too loud because I could see Crystal smirking. I felt like crying.

'I'm sorry, Bea. You're out.'

Chapter Two

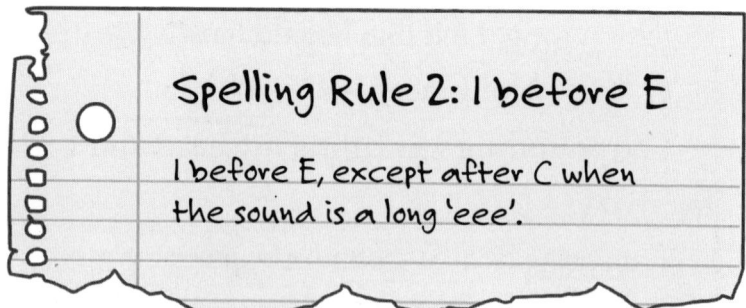

Spelling Rule 2: I before E

I before E, except after C when the sound is a long 'eee'.

This is a rule with lots of exceptions. One exception is the word 'weird' which kind of makes sense: it's the odd one out, the one that doesn't fit in.

Which is exactly how I felt.

Four people made the Spelling Bee team: Crystal, Morven, Kevin Henderson (who kept tapping his feet and fidgeting through the spoken round) and me!

Ms Moon said I came top in the written round. 'You just need to get over those nerves!' she declared, as if that was the easiest thing in the world.

* * *

After school, Morven asked me back to her house to start 'Spell-training'.

Mum said, 'That's really kind, Morven. I'm sure Bea would love to.'

So we walked back together, with Morven chatting non-stop while I just listened. I was worried she was going to trip up, or fall off the pavement, or walk into a lamp-post, but she didn't.

Then we got to her house and she took me through the kitchen and poured glasses of juice. I was seriously beginning to think she didn't have a vision impairment at all, so I asked her how she did it.

'You could get around *your* house in the dark, right?'

I thought about it. 'I reckon I'd bump into things.'

'I do sometimes!' Morven grinned. 'You should see the bruises on my shins.'

'But what about at school?'

'I went in during the holidays and spent loads of time 'mapping' it onto my brain,' she explained. 'It's boring walking round and round the different spaces, and takes ages, but it works. I've actually got a small amount of vision, so I can see fuzzy outlines of stuff. Right now, you look like a blob in front of the fridge.'

I smiled. Being called a blob was better than being called weird, I suppose.

'So, how come you freaked out today?' she said, curiously.

'How could you tell I freaked out?'

'Your voice went all high-pitched and your breathing changed,' said Morven. Then she explained how she can tell what people are feeling from how their voices sound. 'And yours sounded totally freaked out!'

I tried to explain about Crystal – how we used to be friends. 'I could tell she was thinking bad stuff about me.'

'How could you tell?'

'I could just ... see.'

Morven looked puzzled. 'OK, so I can "hear" how people are feeling but how exactly do you "see" someone's thoughts?'

'I don't know ... '

'Perhaps you should just *not* look,' said Morven. 'Try spelling with your eyes closed!'

'Wouldn't that look ... weird?' I said.

Morven shrugged. 'Hey, at least you never have to worry about *me* looking at you weirdly!' She grinned. 'I reckon I might be the perfect friend for you, Spelling Bea!'

Chapter Three

> **Spelling Rule 3: -able or -ible**
>
> If you remove '-able' from a word, you are left with a complete word.
>
> If you remove '-ible' from a word, you are not.
>
> This rule works most (but not all!) of the time.
>
> Exceptions: accessible, digestible, flexible, etc.

After Crystal and I stopped being friends, I felt like an '-ible' word. As if part of me had been taken away and I was no longer complete. That's the only way to describe it.

'You'll make new friends,' Mum said. But how can you be friends with half a person? I felt like an incomplete word. Bea. Or worse, just a letter. B.

Crystal knew everything about me. I always sat in the same place at lunch. I hated being late for lessons. I always put my hand up if I knew the answer and I hated crossing things out in my exercise book. But in Year 4 she started hanging out with some girls who didn't always want to sit in the same place and thought it was fun to be late. 'You don't have to put your hand up *every* time!' she started saying. Or, 'Seriously, just cross that mistake out, Bea!'

She started wearing her hair differently, even though we'd worn our hair the same way since we were in Reception – it was our thing. I didn't change – *she* did. But she said *I* was weird.

* * *

Over the next few days I didn't have time to worry about being weird or being in a new class, because Ms Moon asked me to look after Morven – not that she needed much looking after! It seemed like nothing frightened her. She had only limited vision, but her determination knew no limits, which was amazing.

On day two, we played football in PE and I was wondering how on earth it was going to work.

'We will use a special brightly-coloured ball,' Ms Moon explained.

'Whoa! It jingles too!' said Kevin Henderson.

Ms Moon explained that we would have to communicate while we played. 'Call for the ball and shout the name of the person you're passing to,' she told us. Then she handed out luminous bibs for us all to wear.

'You all look like *bright* blobs now!' Morven declared.

It turned out communicating more made us *all* play better. Morven scored three goals!

On day three, we did a science experiment with a leaf. I was worried Morven wouldn't be able to do it, but she ended up showing *me* because she'd done it at her last school.

On day four, she auditioned for the choir – and got in.

24

Day five: she beat all the footie boys in a keepy-uppy contest.

Day six: she became hula-hooping champion after an epic 100 hula-hoop spin.

By day seven, she was friends with everyone in the school, but for some reason she hung out with me. Every lunchtime, we did 'Spell-training' in the library.

On day eight, Morven suggested we ask Kevin Henderson to join us.

'But he can't sit still! He fidgets *all* the time and plays with a massive ball of rubber bands … he's weird.'

'Isn't that what Crystal called you?'

'Yes, but not weird like Kevin Henderson.'

'Aren't we all a bit weird? Anyway, he's probably just a Rainbow Kid.'

'Rainbow Kid?'

'It's a thing my mum says. She's a child psychologist. She says Rainbow Kids see the world in different colours—'

'Colours?'

'Some people see in blue, or red, or green,' Morven went on. 'Only I reckon we all "see" the world a bit differently. I see blobs and "hear" faces but that doesn't make me weird – just different.'

Not weird but different, I thought. *Am I a Rainbow Kid?*

I wanted to ask more but Kevin Henderson turned up, wriggling like he needed the toilet, or something. 'Can I – um – come in?'

I hadn't spoken two words to Kevin Henderson since Reception, but it turned out he was amazing at spelling. He learned spellings by tapping out the letters on his trouser leg with his fingers. Morven liked to sing the spellings, 'because it helps you learn to spell when you use Braille!'

I told them about some of the spelling rules and we actually had really good fun.

That night, I dreamed of people in different coloured bibs racing up and down a giant rainbow, playing football with a luminous jingly ball, spelling out words as they went. I woke up with a smile on my face.

Chapter Four

> ### Spelling Rule 4: F or PH
>
> The letter F is not allowed in long words.
>
> If a word is long (three or more syllables), then use PH, e.g. geography, biography, peripheral, etc.
>
> As usual, there are exceptions!

After Crystal started hanging out with the other girls, I felt like I was peripheral. Shut out. Not allowed in. Like the letter F, I felt like I didn't belong in big groups. I thought I only belonged in friendships with two people.

Q and U.

Crystal and Bea.

So when Kevin came to join our 'Spell-training', I thought the same thing would happen and I would get pushed out, but I didn't. We worked well as a three. I got better at spelling out loud: Kevin's tapping helped, and Morven made me sing with my eyes shut which felt silly but was fun.

Things were going really well until we turned up for the first round of the competition and straight away I knew it would go wrong.

It was at the town hall, and there were so many people. Six different school teams and a big audience. The bright stage lights made a weird buzzing noise. When I sat down my ears felt clicky and furry like when you have a cold. I wanted to say I couldn't do it, only everyone was clapping: the competition had begun.

'Welcome to the first round of the Spellbinder Competition!' said the judge, a tall woman with maroon hair and green glasses. The lights buzzed, making my head feel prickly and hot. The judge talked about rules and regulations: 'The first round is a play-off. Get a word wrong and you lose a life; get two words wrong and you are out. The two teams with the best scores go to the grand final.'

The words were easy, but I was so nervous the first one came out wrong. I lost a life. Crystal glared at me and I felt the nerves wiping my brain, making me forget every spelling I knew.

'Close your eyes!' whispered Morven.

'Tap your fingers!' advised Kevin.

The words were getting harder. Crystal and Kevin got theirs right. Morven aced her first then messed up on '*risible*' which she spelled with an '-able'. Then it was back to me.

'*Effervescence.*'

I opened my mouth. Nothing came out.

I knew it. Two Fs. *Funny how F is allowed in a long word if it comes with a friend,* I thought.

'I'm going to have to hurry you ... '

I closed my eyes, tapped my fingers.

Nothing.

I was out.

The words got harder. Four schools got knocked out, until it was just Morven, Crystal and Kevin against Ravenswood Grange.

Morven messed up on *'glacier'* (an exception to the I before E rule). Crystal got *'privilege'* wrong (she thought it ended with '-age').

The Ravenswood Grange team were grinning because they knew they were going to be the overall winners. And it was my fault. Suddenly, I felt like my head was going to explode. 'I ... feel sick!'

The next thing I knew, a black curtain was coming down in my head.

Chapter Five

> **Spelling Rule 5: -efy / -ify**
>
> Only four words end in '-efy':
> stupefy, putrefy, rarefy, liquefy.
>
> Memorize those, then use '-ify'
> for all the rest: petrify, clarify,
> beautify, etc.

I like this rule. No exceptions. No grey areas. Just four words – like the four members of our team.

Four people who I had let down.

Four people who lost their chance to win.

Because of me.

The day after I fainted at the competition, I told Mum I felt sick and she let me stay at home. All day, memories of the competition looped through my head and I couldn't make them stop.

After school Morven and Kevin came over, and the first thing I noticed was that Morven was more cautious. 'Tell me if I'm about to crash into a door or go hurtling down some steps!' She flopped down on my bed, laughing. 'Hey, it turns out neither of us is at our best in new places. I suppose that's why you went to pieces yesterday.'

'I didn't go to pieces!'

'You kind of did. Kevin had to stop you falling off the stage when you passed out!'

Kevin looked awkward. 'We still came second. So we got to the final.'

'No thanks to me!' I exclaimed.

'No thanks at all,' Morven agreed. 'Which is why we *really* have to win the whole thing!'

'If we don't, Ms Moon will leave,' said Kevin.

'What?'

'Morven overheard Ms Moon talking to the head teacher in his office.'

'I have supersonic hearing!' Morven laughed. 'OK, not exactly supersonic—'

'She heard Ms Moon saying she'd been offered a job at Ravenswood Grange!'

I thought of the team with the smug smiles. I thought of Ms Moon leaving and my heart sank. Ms Moon, who understood that I liked sitting in the same place. Ms Moon, who learned Braille so she could help Morven. Ms Moon, who let Kevin walk around the room while he did maths.

'If Ravenswood win, she's bound to go and teach there instead,' said Morven.

She was right, but I couldn't go to the final. I told Morven and Kevin that I just couldn't.

'You have to!' said Kevin. 'You're the best speller on the team!

'When I'm not being weird!'

'About that,' said Morven. 'I have an idea!'

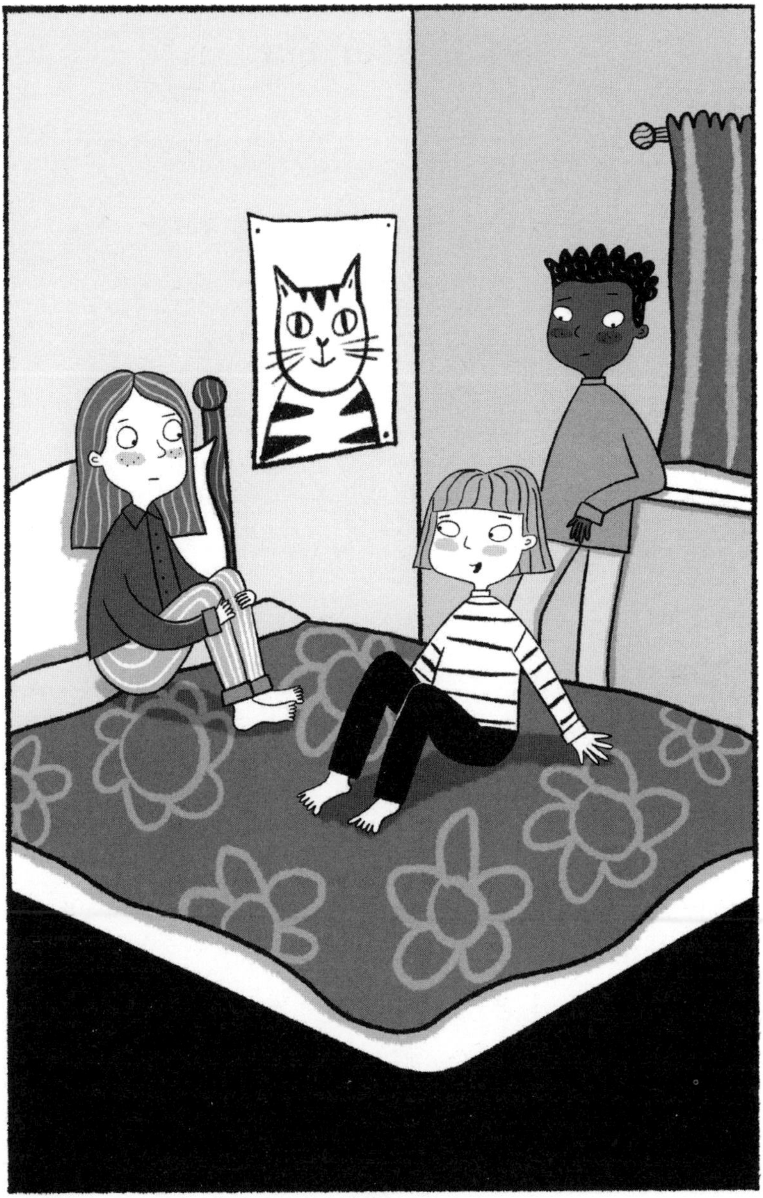

Chapter Six

> **Spelling Rule 6: -ege and -age**
>
> '-ege' occurs in three words: college, privilege, cortege.
>
> Use '-age' for all the rest: language, baggage, mortgage, rummage, damage, etc.

I like exceptions that come in threes. Like me, Kevin and Morven.

'The Three Musketeers,' Kevin called us.

'The Three Degrees,' said Morven.

The Three Amigos, I thought to myself. Because *Amigos* means *Friends*.

Morven's dad took us for a 'mapping' session at Ravenswood Grange, where the final would take place.

'They get home advantage!' complained Kevin.

'That's why I need to figure out the layout and get used to the lights,' explained Morven.

'Do you?' I suspected she might be doing this for my benefit.

'I do actually! New spaces are difficult when you have a vision impairment. And stage lights confuse me – especially fluorescent or flickery ones.'

I looked at her in surprise. She seemed to take everything in her stride.

'But we're also doing it for you!' she admitted. 'I got you these as well.'

She produced two orange foam blobs. 'Ear plugs. I use them for sensory overload.'

'Sensory what?'

'Supersonic hearing gets a bit much in noisy spaces. These muffle the sound. They might help you too.'

'And I got you this!' said Kevin, handing me a ball of rubber bands. 'I find it easier to focus when I'm fiddling. It was Ms Moon's idea.'

'That's really … ' I wanted to say 'weird' but instead I said, 'nice. Thank you, Kevin.'

We checked out the stage and the technician turned on the lights for us. Then Morven grabbed me and Kevin and made us dance in the spotlight. At first I felt really silly but by the end we were all laughing so much we nearly toppled off the stage.

On the way home, Morven said, 'One more thing. You and Crystal have to sort things out before the final. You only mess up spellings when she's around!'

'But ... what do I say?'

'Just ask why she stopped being friends with you!' said Morven. 'Then you'll know once and for all.'

Was she right? Or was it better not knowing? The idea of talking to Crystal made me feel sick. I wasn't sure I could do it.

Chapter Seven

> Spelling Rule 7: fore- and for-
>
> Start your word with 'fore-' to mean before or ahead: forefather, forecast, foresight, etc.
>
> Otherwise start with 'for-': forbid, forfeit, forlorn, forget ... forgive.

It snowed on the day of the final. Some people like snow but I don't. It changes everything. The car journey was slower, and my shoes got wet, and the venue smelled different – even the light was different.

Morven had a white cane, to help her manage the unfamiliar space, and she wore pink sparkly sunglasses to help with the stage lighting.

The white cane showed everyone she had a vision impairment. *Did she mind looking different?* I wondered.

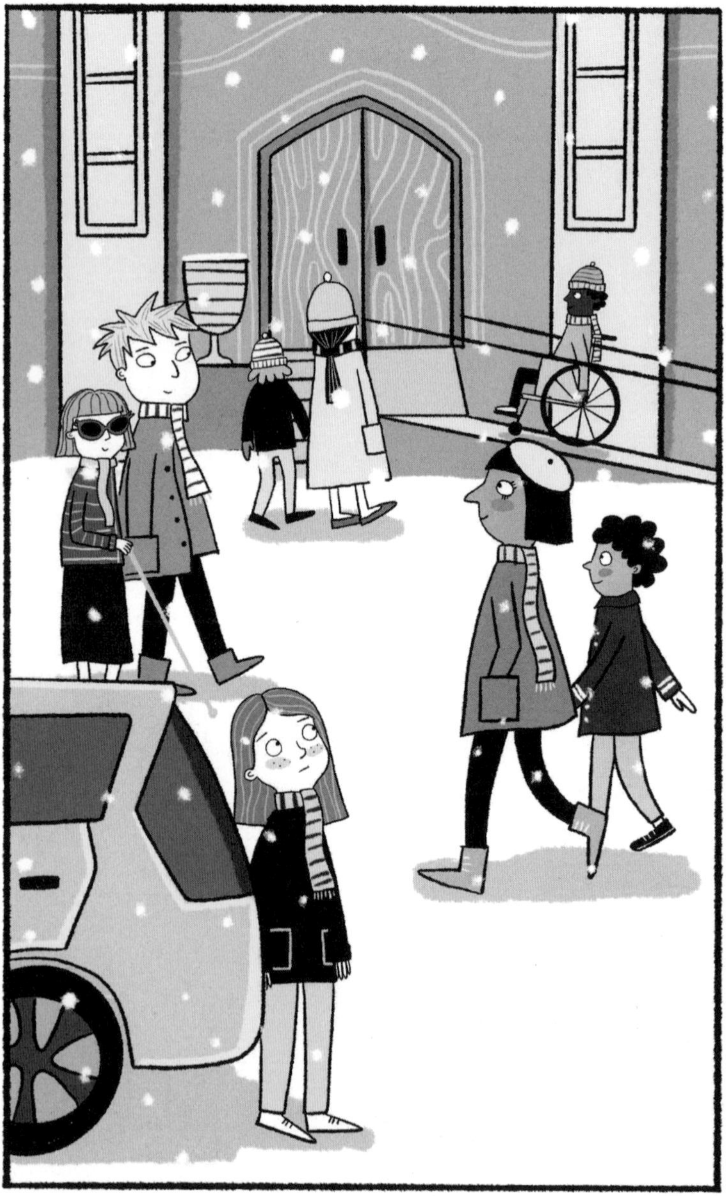

Morven rummaged in her bag and produced three more sparkly pairs of glasses for the team.

'But won't we look ... weird?' I asked.

'Who cares?' she said. 'Sometimes the bravest thing is to admit you need help. Now, you need to go and talk to Crystal before the competition starts.'

'Now?'

'Now!'

Morven and Kevin grabbed me by the arms and dragged me towards Crystal. 'Bea wants to know why you aren't friends anymore,' Morven said.

Crystal looked surprised. 'Um – don't *you* know? I mean, *you* stopped talking to *me*.'

'Because you made friends with all the other girls,' I said quietly.

'Yes, but I was still friends with you too ... until you kept going off.'

Suddenly I felt like I was going to cry. 'I thought you didn't want me around.'

'Why would you think that?'

'You said I was weird!'

Crystal frowned. 'No, I said you were *being* weird. Because you stopped talking to me – even looking at me – I didn't know why.'

There were tears in my eyes and everything looked blurry.

'And then you made friends with Morven and Kevin and you didn't ask me to come to practice with you ... '

'I didn't think you wanted to!'

Crystal shrugged. 'You didn't ask.'

Now I saw she was crying too. And although everything looked fuzzy, for the first time I saw everything in a whole new light.

Then the stage lights went up and the final began.

Chapter Eight

> ### Spelling Rule 8: -tch or -ch
>
> Use 'tch' if it comes after a single vowel: catch, fetch, watch, etc.
>
> Use '-ch' if it comes after a consonant or two vowels: bench, church, approach, etc.
>
> But there are many exceptions to this rule: detach, enrich, much, sandwich, spinach …

I never used to like rules with lots of exceptions because they confused me. I didn't like standing out and being different. But it turns out lots of people are exceptions. Lots of people are different – in their own way.

'Remember: nerves are a good thing!' Ms Moon told us before the competition.

'They raise your heart rate which pumps more blood to your brain. Nerves can help you – if you let them! Now go out and smash this!'

'If we don't win, will you go and teach at Ravenswood Grange?' Morven blurted out.

Ms Moon laughed. 'Of course not – whatever gave you that idea? Win or lose, you are my superstar spellers, and I am so proud of you!'

As the lights went up, I saw her grinning at me from the audience and I really wanted to win this for her – and for Morven and Kevin. And Crystal.

So that day, I used my nerves and found my voice. The earplugs definitely helped me focus on the questions, instead of the audience. The funny pink sunglasses blocked out the glare of the lights. I had Kevin's ball of rubber bands in my pocket. And though I was still nervous, I tried to remember that these were good nerves.

We aced the early rounds, knocking out two rival teams. I got every single spelling right and with one round to go, it was between us and Ravenswood Grange.

The judge spoke solemnly into her microphone. 'Please select one team member for the head-to-head round.'

'It has to be you, Bea!' whispered Kevin.

'You are absolutely on fire!' said Morven.

'And totally our best speller!' added Crystal.

Suddenly the wrong kind of nerves threatened to overwhelm me again. 'I don't think I can do it on my own.'

'You won't be on your own,' stated Morven.

'We'll all be right behind you!' said Kevin.

I turned to Crystal. 'All of you?'

She smiled. 'All of us.'

'And maybe – after the competition – we can be friends again?'

'I was always your friend,' said Crystal. 'You just couldn't see it.'

Chapter Nine

> Spelling Rule 9: z / zz
>
> When z appears at the beginning of a word, it is on its own – zoo, zebra, zenith, etc.
>
> When it appears at the end of a word, it has found a friend – buzz, whizz, fuzz, etc.

I got all the words right, one after another. I didn't stumble or hesitate. I tapped them out with my fingers, and I sing-songed them in my head. I remembered the rules – and the exceptions – because that was my way of doing it. The captain of the Ravenswood team was really good too and we were on exactly the same score going into the tie-break final.

But then a teacher from Ravenswood was whispering something to the judge.

'I'm afraid I'm going to have to ask Bea to remove her ear devices,' she declared.

'But they're just earplugs!' Kevin objected.

'And your glasses need to come off, too. There has been a suggestion they may be "wired up" – or wireless – or some such.'

'This is ridiculous!' said Ms Moon, glaring at the Ravenswood teacher.

I was about to say that I couldn't do it without them. After all, Morven said it was OK to admit you need a little help. But she also showed me that it was OK to take risks and to trust yourself.

'It's OK,' I said. 'I know I can do this.'

The Ravenswood captain was good, but I knew I could beat him. When he stumbled on the easy 'I before E' rule, I knew I had a chance to win the trophy for our team.

I just needed to get the next word right. One word.

'*Soliloquy.*'

Time slowed down.

I knew what the word meant: a soliloquy is a speech delivered by one person on stage. On their own.

But it has a Q in the middle. And a U. Because even when you think you are on your own – all alone on a big stage with an audience staring up at you – you have friends, right there beside you. Crystal had been my friend all along. I just hadn't seen it. And now I had three friends. Standing silent beside me, like the U in *soliloquy*, all willing me to get it right.

I took a deep breath. 'S –O – L – I'

The lights felt super bright and the silence was intense and everyone in the audience was looking at me. What could they see? A girl who gets nervous sometimes. Who doesn't like change and loves to play by the rules. A girl who is really, really good at spelling.

'L – O'

I thought of Morven – the girl who made me 'see' the world through new eyes. She had showed me how to be brave – and that it's also OK to ask for help.

After this competition is over, I thought, *I'm going to spend time with my friends. Maybe even make some new ones. Because I'm Bea. And the letter B gets on with all sorts of other letters, whether they are vowels or consonants. B works in words with one syllable, or lots of syllables. It's a letter with a lot of friends.*

It just sees the world a little differently.

'Q – U – Y!'